Nestlé®

smarties®

HOW TO DRAW
CARTOONS

David Mostyn has been drawing
and illustrating books and comics
for many years. Here are just a few
of them:

Smarties Joke Book
The Joke Museum
1001 Animal Quackers
Beano and Dandy
Smarties Incredible Facts
The Biggest Joke Book
in the World

HOW TO DRAW CARTOONS

David Mostyn

Robinson Children's Books

First published in the UK by Robinson Children's Books,
an imprint of Constable & Robinson Ltd, 2000

Constable & Robinson Ltd
3 The Lanchesters
162 Fulham Palace Road
London
W6 9ER

A copy of the British Library Cataloguing in Publication Data for this title
is available from the British Library.

ISBN 1 - 84119 - 0151 - 5

Printed and bound in the EC

10 9 8 7 6 5 4 3 2 1

Contents

CHAPTER ONE
Getting Started

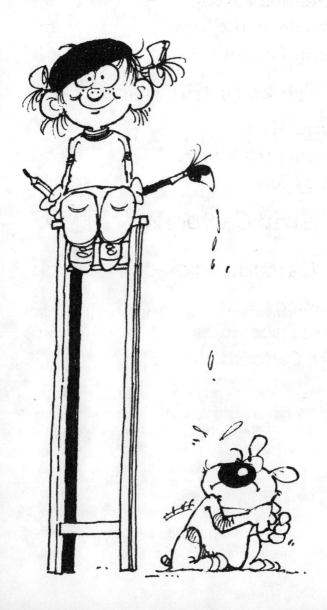

Drawing cartoons is such fun, I like to think everyone can do it if they try. And if you haven't tried or been able to before now, I believe my book will show you how – easily. It's the no fuss method to drawing cartoons!

The equipment you need is simple and inexpensive. I'm going to describe the tools I use. They're the ones that I find suit me best and the way I work.

You may find that you prefer a softer pencil, or a different type of paper. Experiment with different materials as combinations of materials give different effects. When you feel happy with your equipment, try to stick with it, as practice will improve results.

There is a huge range of equipment on the market. A lot of it is very similar, and a lot of it is gimmicky. Keep your equipment simple!

The Tools of the Trade

PAPER

There are basically two kinds of cartoons: those in black and white (b/w) and those in colour. For b/w work, try a harder, smoother paper such as Bristol Board or line Board. These harder papers will give you a clean solid black line.

For colour work, you have to find a paper that will enable you to draw a clean black line, and at the same time accept colour. Try to use Hot Press (HP) papers, these are smooth watercolour papers, which are the type that I use.

PENCILS

Some pencils are softer than others. Near one end of a pencil you will find one or two letters or numbers. HB stands for Hard Black. So if you see you have a 5H pencil, it will be very hard. If you have a 5B pencil, it will be very soft. I usually work with one between 2B and 4B. If you are doing a lot of drawing, you may find a conventional pencil is a nuisance because you have to keep sharpening it. Clutch pencils are an excellent substitute, and do not need sharpening.

ERASURES

Conventional erasures are not a good way of cleaning a drawing as they can remove the surface of the paper. Putty rubbers, which look a bit like Blu-Tack, are a much better option as they only remove pencil marks.

PENS

If you want to achieve a good crisp, black ink line the best thing to use is a dip-pen, but they can be difficult to master and they are quite difficult to find. If you do decide to use a dip-pen my advice would be to try a broader, less 'sharp' nib, such as a 303. The larger the nib, the less likely it is to 'catch' in the paper.

Using a nib does take practice but you can achieve wonderful results, especially as a dip-pen is very flexible, which means you are able to draw an interesting, flexible line.

Felt pens are also excellent to use. They come in varying thickness and deliver a reasonably 'black' line, but I don't think they will ever be as good as ink.

BRUSHES

There are many different makes, shapes and sizes of brushes on the market. I use two types of brush. The first is a number (nos.) 6, for colour. The second is a number 2 for black ink only, as black ink is very difficult to remove from a brush, and can muddy other colours. Try a size that will suit you, and stick to it. You might like to buy a nos. 10 or 12 for putting on large areas of wash.

It is almost impossible to clean black ink out of a brush entirely and you will find that as the deposits of ink build up over time, the bristles will spread, and you'll have to throw the brush away. Mine last about two months, but I'm drawing many hours each day.

COLOUR

Find a black ink you are happy with. Black ink can get a bit gluey in hot weather so store it in a cool place. Be very careful handling it as once it gets on your clothes, it can be very difficult to remove. A useful tip is to use a small bottle that can be easily refilled.

I use two types of colour and both are water-based. The first are just straightforward watercolour pans. I bought an empty box, and then filled it with a range of colours that suited me. Watercolours are soft and reasonably easy to use, but they do tend to reproduce in a very 'soft' way, i.e. pale.

The second type of colours are coloured inks. These are very strong, clear colours; ideal for strip cartoons and comic work.

There are, of course, many other colouring materials and technologies. Materials such as pastel and crayon are not ideally suited to a cartoon technique, which generally relies on flat, bright colours. The main things to remember are that you need bright, clean colours that dry quickly and flat.

And don't forget white paint – it can be very useful for whiting out mistakes or putting in highlights.

COMPUTER COLOURING

Many cartoons are now coloured using a computer. The only point you should try to remember when you're drawing a cartoon that is going to be coloured by this method, is to make sure that the lines are all 'joined up'. If they are not, the colour you want in a particular area may flood the whole area of the cartoon. You should check this anyway by quickly scanning your line drawing for breaks, before you start.

OTHER BITS AND PIECES

I have found that it's more convenient to draw on a board that has a slight slope, but many people prefer to work on a flat top.

You will need a millimetre ruler and try to buy quite a long one. Mine are between 300 and 400 mm long. Rulers usually come in plastic or steel, but I prefer plastic as steel sometimes marks the paper.

A good set of compasses is useful to help with all those circles you'll be drawing – try and find one with a ruling pen extension which will allow you to draw circles in ink or paint.

Light boxes are extremely useful if you need to trace your roughs.

PLACE OF WORK

Even if you work in ideal conditions – a beautiful studio with north-facing light – you will also need additional light to ensure excellent visibility.

Make sure you have plenty of space and light, clear the table, sharpen your pencil and, if you're going to be sitting at your drawing board for long periods, make sure you have a comfortable and supportive chair.

Okay – you're ready, and well equipped to draw. Let's see what you can do!

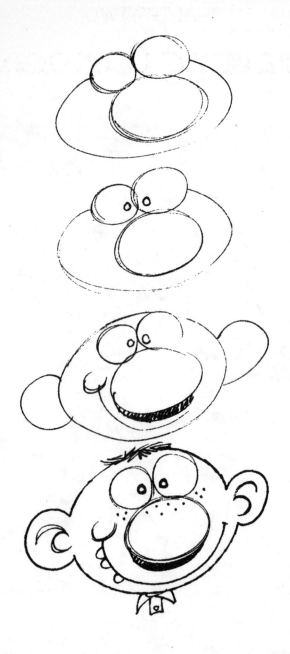

CHAPTER TWO
Drawing Cartoons

Many people seem to fall into the trap of thinking of a cartoon as a casually drawn 'funny picture', scribbled down on a piece of paper. But they forget that most of the time a cartoon is being drawn for a reason, usually to help to tell a story. First decide what you want to draw, then with a little practice you'll be able to build your cartoon from a few basic ingredients.

Funny Faces

So start with the basic drawing of ... a head

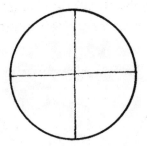

add the eyes

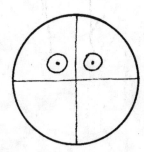

then the nose

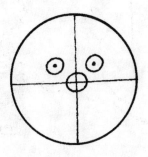

and finally the mouth.

Change the expression by moving the position of the pupils in the eyes

or the shape of the mouth.

Now comes the fun bit – start to add hair and eyebrows…

Remember always to begin with the same
construction.

Try altering one feature and see how easily it is to
change the look of the whole face.

Now try and change all the features and see how many expressions you can make.

The next step is to change the shape of the head.

If you change the expressions on each of the different shapes you will find that you will emphasise the character of the cartoons. For example,

Dracula

School boy

Thug

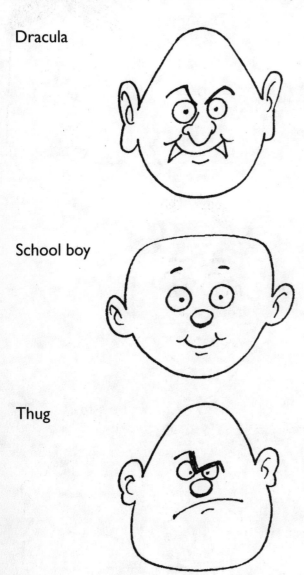

Don't forget that by drawing suitable hair, etc. on the face, you can add to the general effect:

Thick hair

Curly hair

Hardly any hair

Cartoons are really an exaggeration of reality, so start to think how you can improve on your faces, keeping this point in mind.

Use existing drawings and exaggerate some of the features.

Nodding Heads

If you want to move your heads, it is very simple. As usual, begin with your basic construction. But instead of drawing the eyes and nose in a central position … move them around the face, and you will find the head moves.

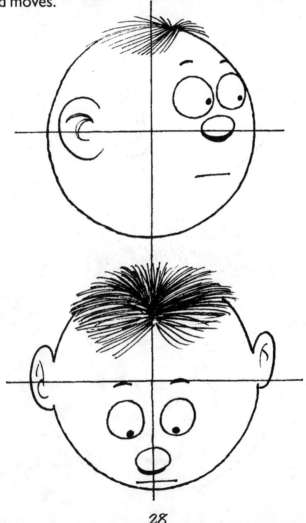

When you have moved the position, think of what expressions would be suitable and see how it transforms your simple faces into cartoons.

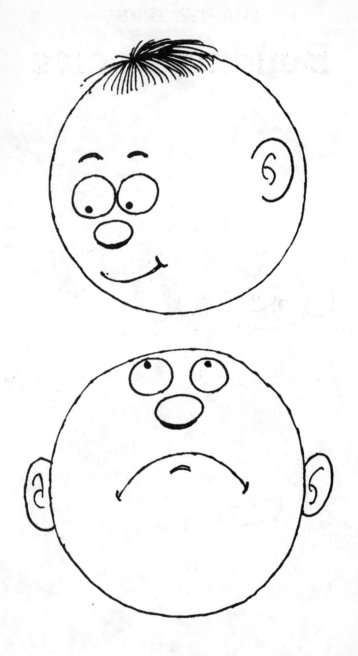

CHAPTER THREE

Building Bodies

The Main Bit

We begin on the body. The human body has hundreds of muscles and bones, and every human body looks slightly different. The good news is that to draw a good cartoon, all you have to do is to draw a series of different-sized sausages.

YUMMY!

This is the basic body shape and by altering the size and shape of the sausages you can see how easy it is to change it. So for a huge, tall, fat person you draw this.

For a tall, skinny person, change it to this.

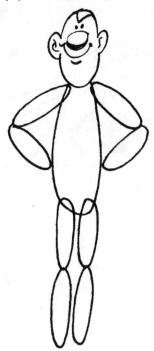

A small, skinny person looks like this.

A tremendously strong person looks like this.

The End Bits

Hands and feet are difficult to draw and it takes a great deal of practice to draw them well. Because of this, it is even more important to try to begin with a basic construction.

Here are examples of hands and feet in various positions. Copy or trace these drawings and then try drawing them in different positions. The more you draw them the better you can become.

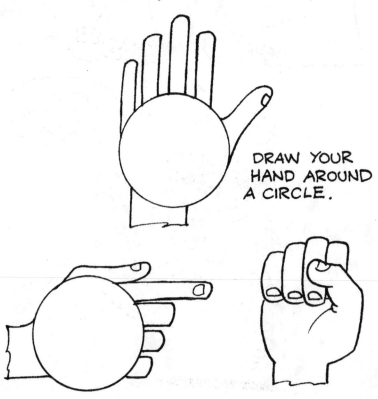

DRAW YOUR HAND AROUND A CIRCLE.

The Whole Thing

CHAPTER FOUR
Amazing Animals

All Shapes and Sizes

Now you understand how to draw a basic cartoon figure, you can use the same method for drawing animals. Of course, like humans, animals come in every shape and size imaginable, but in general they all have four legs, the same basic construction of face, and tails of different lengths, thickness and colour.

The Eyes, Snout and Mouth

The position of all the elements on an animal's face is, broadly speaking, the same. Once you have understood this, you can vary the shape and size of these elements, depending on which animal you are drawing.

Begin with the basic construction, as before. The head is constructed exactly the same as a human head, with one simple difference.

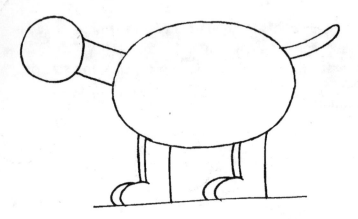

Where the nose is on a human, on an animal there is a snout, with a nose on the end of that.

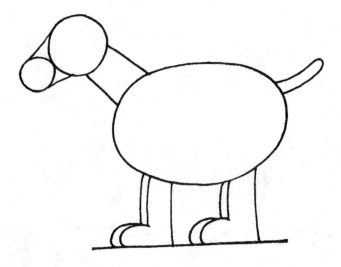

This is broadly true of all animals – some snouts are shorter and fatter, some are longer and narrower.

Put in eyes exactly as for humans, and use the same techniques to draw the expressions.

The mouth goes along the bottom of the snout, and the ears move to the top of the head.

Changing Shape

Now you have the basic construction, try and vary the size of each part of the body.

As you can see, as soon as you start changing its parts, you can begin to imagine which animal the drawing could closest resemble.

So by making the right changes to the basic body you can draw lots of different animals quite easily. You can improve the drawing if you take the basic shape one step further.

Instead of the body being just one oval sausage, make it into two circles, the front one being larger.

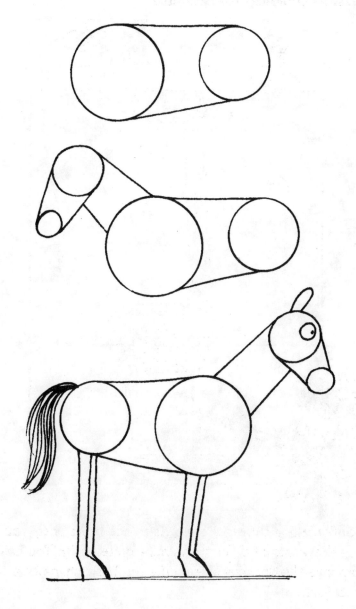

Even for professional artists, animals are sometimes not very easy to imagine. Try looking at pictures of them or studying your own pets.

Let's try all this out on a few animals.

Make a pig very fat.

Try a dog.

Here are a few more animals with the construction lines drawn in. (Draw these lines in pencil and then remove them after you've inked in.)

You can begin to see that animals are all built in the same way. Find a good picture of your animal, draw the basic construction using circles and sausages, and try to get as near to the real thing as possible. Then take the outstanding characteristic of that animal and really exaggerate it. Make a pig really fat, a lion super fierce, a little bug really horrible, and so on. Go on, try it!

Prehistoric Cartoons

Dinosaurs and monsters are also great fun to draw because they all look so weird it's a great opportunity to exaggerate some features even more.

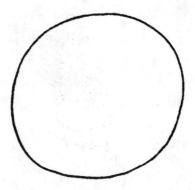

As always we start with a simple construction

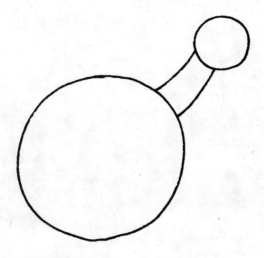

Add the legs and the snout

then the scales and a long tail.

CHAPTER FIVE
Animal Moods

We're going to use exactly the same set of rules we applied to drawing human faces and draw some amazing animals' faces. As I explained earlier on in the book, most animals have snouts instead of noses.

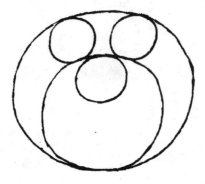

This is a basic face. If you want to draw a particular animal, find a good picture, say of a lion, and then adapt the basic face.

If we change the expression we can change our nice friendly lion in to a nasty fierce lion.

Let's try the same approach with a totally different animal – an elephant.

If we change what the elephant is doing we can change his mood to a frightened elephant.

Never hesitate to find pictures or reference material from which you can draw your figures. It's certainly not cheating. Many professional artists and cartoonists use models and photographs as reference. You'd be a genius if you could keep it all in your head.

The next chapter is all about how to make things move.

CHAPTER SIX
Action Cartoons

Get Moving

Get up from the chair in which you are enjoying every golden moment of this book and walk across the room. Unless you're a frog, you might have noticed that when your left arm swings forward, so does your right leg. So when you draw your cartoon walking it needs to do the same ...

If you want to draw it from the front, it should look like this. Make the front foot and hand larger to emphasise the movement.

Faster and Faster

The same thing happens when the figure is running, only the arms and legs are raised higher, and the body slopes forward.

The position of the body will give some idea of speed. To make it look faster make the figure slope further forwards.

Or move upright for a gentle jog.

Animals on the Run

When you come to draw an animal moving, you're in real trouble.

Some animals change the rhythm of their legs when they walk, or run, or canter. Some animals even walk differently from others.

This is the great advantage of being a cartoonist –
there's no need to be realistic. Because there are so
many variations, we can turn it to our advantage and
make the animals look funny when they move.

Or you can quite simply make them move like humans.

Action Packed

The human figure can make lots of very different and difficult movements. Unless you want to read 672 more pages on movement of the human body, I'm only going to show you how to get started.

First decide on your action. Let's say a person is kicking a ball. Either get a friend actually to do it for you, that is, kick a ball for you, or find a picture of a ball being kicked. I sometimes do the action myself to see how my arms and legs move. Make sure no one's watching – they might think you're a bit mad! Make a quick scribble to see if it looks correct.

Using this rough scribble, build up your figure over it.
Don't try to make it a cartoon at this stage.

Add a few more features, such as hair, eyebrows and details to the clothes. When you are reasonably happy, you can make a clean drawing of your rough sketch.

To make a good clean drawing, tape your scribble to a light box. Put a fresh sheet of paper on top and you will see your first drawing clearly through it. Now trace round the figure. If you think the drawing is still a bit wrong, repeat the process with another piece of clean paper, correcting the drawing as you go. You should end up with a reasonably accurate drawing of your figure.

Now you have a correct drawing you can begin to turn into a cartoon.

If you want to make him super tough add big boots, less hair and big muscles …

Now try the same with a dainty skater.

So don't forget – plan your action, make a quick rough, correct it if you feel you have to, and then start turning it into a cartoon, using all the expertise you've acquired in the previous chapters!

CHAPTER SEVEN

Tricks of the Trade

Helpful Hints

The art of cartooning is no exception when it comes to 'tricks of the trade'. Here are a few hints to play around with. They will make your drawings look a lot more alive.

When the figure is running along it helps to put in a few extras for maximum effect – a few speed lines perhaps.

Another trick is to put a shadow under the figure.

How about putting everything in – dust, lines, and shadows!

If the cartoon figure hits something, here's how you can show it.

Now say, for example, a fist is coming out to punch you. Draw the fist in the middle of a circle.

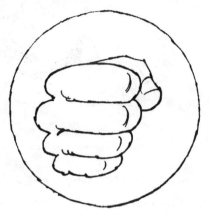

Add some impact

Here's another way to show it.

Another trick is to show action from beginning to end.

This is much more exciting.

Anything that helps to show action in a cartoon must be a bonus. But be very careful not to put in so much that the whole thing becomes confused – a mish-mashed jumble of lines. Too little is better than too much.

You can make all the parts of your cartoon reflect the fact that the ball is hitting him on the head.

Words are also a very effective way to show action.

Always plan out carefully what you are going to do. The effect might *look* very casually done, but it must be planned and drawn with great care.

Start with a rough sketch

then add some exaggeration.

You can invent your own words, and if you can't think of ways to draw them, look in any good comic and see how the cartoonists there achieve their effects.

Practice really does make perfect so have a go and
try to invent some of your own ideas and techniques.
Never be afraid to experiment!

Building the Picture

Before you start, here are a few hints about composition. When you've sorted out in your mind what it is you are going to draw, make a very quick scribble of it. Let's say, a man running down a road.

Now imagine you're a camera moving around that man, looking for the best angle. It could be down very low, or up high, or from the back, or dead-on from the front. Decide on your angle and draw it.

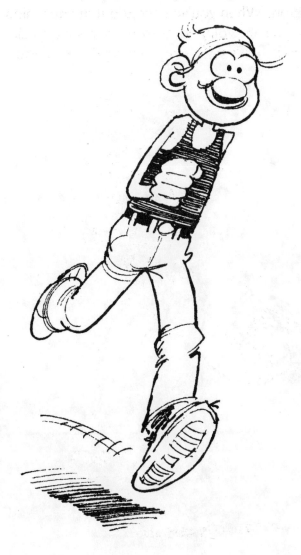

Now to make it even more outstanding, try placing it in a frame. Draw a frame on a separate piece of paper and move it around until you think you have the best look to it. You can even draw him bursting out of the frame.

Don't forget, suit the composition to the subject you're drawing. For example, if you want to show the approach of a sinister figure, you could make it look very dramatic by drawing the figure quite small in the frame, and rather dark or even in silhouette.

So always try to go for an unusual angle, and think how it would look its best within the frame of a picture.

Loony Tunes

You need to know about drawing things that don't move, as much as those that do! For instance, suppose you've done a wonderful cartoon of someone riding a bike. The person riding the bike may look very funny, but what about the bike? You can't make a bike look 'funny', but you can make it look 'cartoony'. One very simple way to do this is to make a correct drawing of a bike and then put an overlay over the first drawing and redraw it at top speed. Exaggerate some of it's parts and give it speed lines.

Now try and make the same bike move

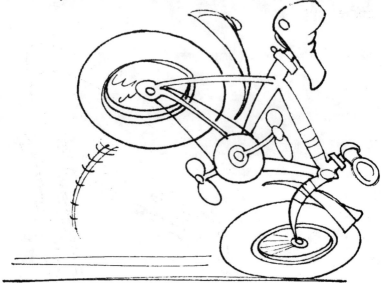

Or make it look angry.

Although this is a correct drawing of a bike, it does take on a cartoon quality.

Now try and apply this to any object and see how it comes out.

A car...

A hammer...

A kettle...

A flower – with a face, of course! That's the great thing about cartoons, the more you distort them, the better they look.

And an apple…

…can even become scary.

CHAPTER EIGHT
Strip Cartoons

Strips are very popular – almost everyone at some time or other has read them in some form. They're always very easy to read and that's because, in general, the writers and artist try to stick to a set of rules that helps the reader.

A strip cartoon is produced by a writer, and/or an artist. The writer is the person responsible for coming up with the idea, and then writing it down in a way that's clear and explanatory for the artist. There is a very brief description of the action followed by the words that the characters say to each other.

Here is a typical example of a script.

FISHY SID

1. Sid and his pal Joey are off for a day's fishing.
   Sid: Light breeze, cloudy, not too hot, perfect for fishing.
   Joey: Yep!

2. At the river bank the two friends settle down to the serious business of fishing.
   Sid: I'm going to try for the club record!
   Joey: Me too, so watch out!

3. Sid is making his first cast while Joey looks on.
   Sid: Here goes!

4. A sudden strong gust of wind blows Sid's line and tangles up Joey.
   Joey: Hey. Watch what you're doing.

5. Sid has untangled Joey and now they both begin to fish in earnest. Later.
   Sid: This time I mean business.
   Joey: Just watch which way you're going, Sid.

6. But again, another strong gust catches the line and this time the two chums are really caught.
   Joey: Bah. What did I tell you, you pest!
   Sid: Gulp. But I don't understand it. There's no wind!

7. While the two untangle themselves, their rival, Percy Pike, now appears on the opposite bank, and we can see that he has been holding a huge fan that he has been using to blow Sid's line away from the river.

   Percy: Hah, hah, hah! Now I'm going to get the club record while my FANS watch!

8. Sid and Joey untangle themselves while Percy catches fish.

   Sid: That bully. I'll put a stop to his pranks.

9. We now see that Percy has caught a huge fish and is really having a terrific fight.

   Percy: I've caught the record fish this time!

10. Percy has now landed a huge horrible-looking monster fish. The fish is now attacking him.

    Monster: GRRR! SNAP! CRUNCH! ROAR!

    Percy: Help! It's going to get me!

11. Percy is last seen heading off into the distance. The monster turns out to be Sid dressed up. Joey looks on.

    Sid: Ho, ho, ho! Percy may have made a good catch, but we've got it in the bag!

    Joey: Hah, hah, hah! That'll teach the bully to tangle with us!

END

The first thing to do is to think up a storyline that has plenty of scope for building in lots of jokes and ideas. Try, as far as possible, to keep the number of characters in the storyline down to a minimum. In the story about Fishy Sid, we have two main characters and one bad guy. You can always bring in other people to suit the story but there should always be two or three main characters. Always keep the speech down to an absolute minimum. Always move the action and the speech from left to right, the way we read. Never have one of the characters saying more than one thing in the frame.

When you come to drawing out the strip, decide on your finished size, and then draw it twice the size to give yourself more room.

FINISHED SIZE

YOUR DRAWING SIZE

When you draw in your cartoons, start in pencil and sketch out the whole thing.

Try to vary the scene you are showing as much as possible, and always look for an interesting way or angle to show it.

So always look for an exciting and different angle on the picture. When you've finished the drawing in pencil, fill it in with black ink and then go back and put in the solid areas of black that you think will help to make the strip look more dramatic. Keep your drawing towards the bottom two-thirds of each frame to allow for speech bubbles.

HERE, THERE'S PLENTY OF SPACE FOR SPEECH BUBBLES, AND THE ACTION IS MOVING FROM LEFT TO RIGHT.

If you find you have plenty of room in the frame for your speech bubbles, then try using an oval to draw round the text.

If you're fairly tight for space, a box will fit in more easily.

Always try to make the leader line from the speech bubble point at the mouth of the person who's talking. Look at the work of other cartoonists – there's plenty of reference around. Study how they draw their strips.

Why not try and do your own strip cartoon for Fishy Sid?

CHAPTER NINE

Cartoon Projects

Cartoons are great fun to draw, but how about making use of this new talent.

Greetings Cards

Creating cards for other people is always great fun. Find out as much as you can about the subject of the card before you begin. Plan out what you are going to do and link it up with a funny message to go inside. If you intend to send the card in an envelope, just find a suitably sized envelope first – before you cut the paper on which you'll be drawing.

Party Decorations

If you're going to decorate a room for a party, find out what the theme is going to be. Let's say it's a 'ghosts and ghouls' party. I think that it's always better to have too many decorations than too few.

If you want to draw horrible spiders coming down from the ceiling, draw and make just one…

Don't forget the spider needs eight legs

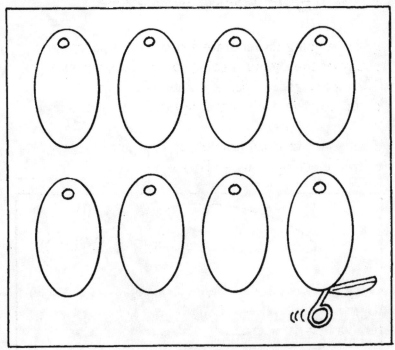

Use string or cotton thread to attach the legs

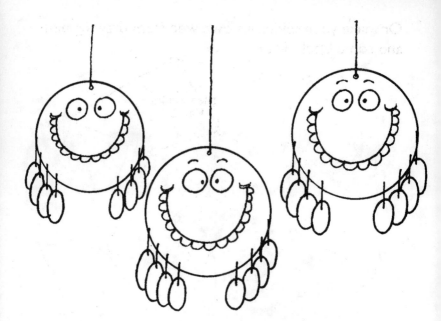

Once you've assembled one item, you can get a team together and, using your spider as a guide, produce quite a few nasty creepy crawlies in no time at all.

You can hang lots of them from the ceiling ...

Or make your spider it's own web from drawing pins and some black wool.

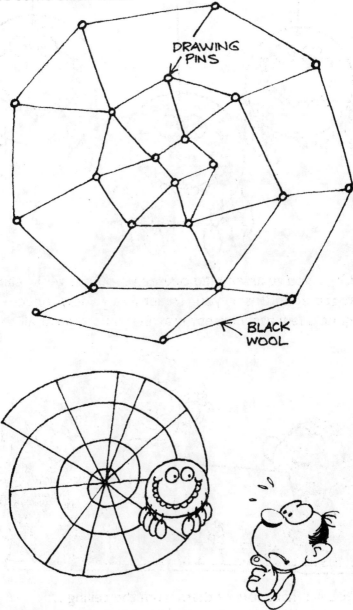

Use your new skills to draw a mask or a skeleton.

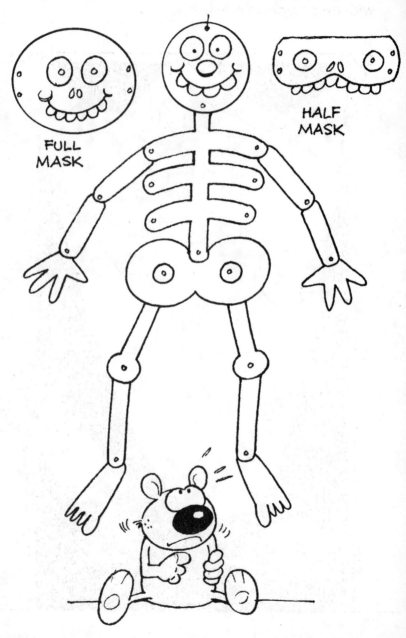

FULL
MASK

HALF
MASK

You can hang blankets in ghostly ways over doors with eyes stuck on them.

Carry the theme through all the decorations: black balloons, skeletons, spider webs. It helps a great deal if you have a couple of friends to help you with ideas. One thing to remember is that if you're making this type of decoration for a small child, don't make it too frightening! I know from experience that you can overwhelm a child guest who is too afraid to enter the 'party room' because he is terrified of the decorations! Have fun!

Huge Cartoons

If you have a class project to do and you want to draw cartoons on a very large scale, here are a couple of ways to do it. If you feel confident, spread your sheet of paper out on the floor or wall and draw it out as you would normally. Just make sure you plan it all out using a very soft pencil that can be easily rubbed out when you've finished.

Another way is to draw your normal size of cartoon and draw a grid over it. Then draw another grid with the same number of squares twice as big.

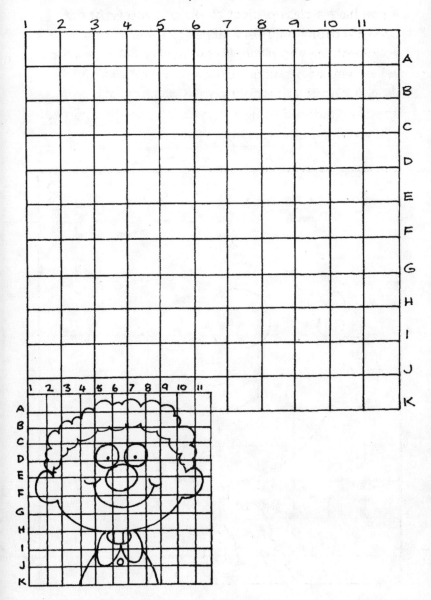

Now simply take each square in order, from left to right, and draw in on the large square what you see in the equivalent smaller square. It will automatically enlarge itself. At this stage it is a good idea to try to rub out as many of the grid lines as you can. Try it, it's a very simple and effective technique. Many of the great painters of the past have used this method to do their paintings on walls and ceilings.

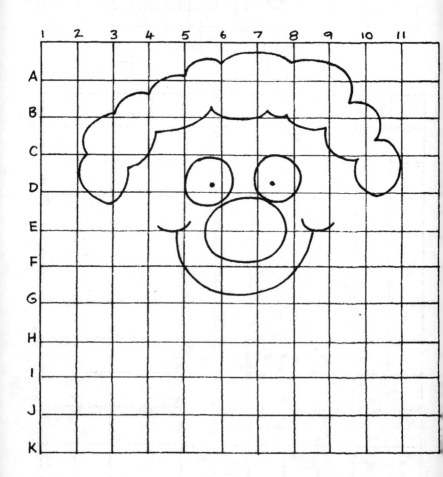

You can use the same technique for any type of picture. Try this one.

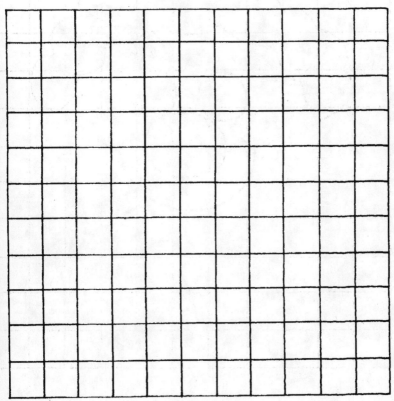

It's also very useful for painting scenery, particularly as once you have drawn the picture, you can ask friends to help you colour it all in.

Happy drawing!

Smarties Books are:

Fun, colourful, interactive, imaginative, creative, wacky and there's lots in them.

Other books available

Smarties Incredible Facts ☐

Colourful, fun and packed with totally unbelievable facts, suitable for ages 6 – 64.
ISBN: 1 8114 068 3
Price: £6.99

Smarties Joke Book ☐

This will keep you laughing for years, the ultimate joke book ever published.
ISBN: 1 84119 069 1
Price: £3.99

ONLY SMARTIES ® HAVE THE ANSWER

Smarties Smart Science ☐

An unique approach to science – to prove it is fun.
ISBN: 1 84119 150 7
Price: £3.99

Robinson books are available from all good bookshops or direct from the publishers.
Just tick the titles you want and fill in the form below.

TBS Direct
Colchester Road, Frating Green, Colchester, Essex CO7 7DW Tel: +44 (0) 1206 255777
Fax: +44 (0) 1206 255914 Email: sales@tbs-ltd.co.uk

UK/BFPO customers please allow £1.00 for p&p for the first book, plus 50p for the
second, plus 30p for each additional book up to a maximum charge of £3.00.
Please send me the titles ticked.
Overseas customers (inc. Ireland), please allow £2.00 for the first book, plus £1.00 for the
second, plus 50p for each additional book.
NAME (Block letters)...
ADDRESS...
....
POSTCODE..
I enclose a cheque/PO (payable to TBS Direct) for..
I wish to pay by Switch/Credit card...
Number..
Card Expiry Date...
Switch Issue Number...